Original title:
Tropical Escape Routes

Copyright © 2025 Creative Arts Management OÜ
All rights reserved.

Author: Evan Hawthorne
ISBN HARDBACK: 978-1-80581-607-2
ISBN PAPERBACK: 978-1-80581-134-3
ISBN EBOOK: 978-1-80581-607-2

Gentle Waves and Golden Sands

A beach ball bounces high and far,
While seagulls squawk like they're some stars.
Children dig deep, searching for gold,
But all they find is a crusty old mold.

Sunscreen's slathered in a big, thick layer,
Now everyone's looking like a wet player.
Laughter echoes with each splash and dive,
As we pretend that we're all alive!

Chasing Fireflies at Dusk

Under the stars, we run and we trip,
Collecting glow bugs for a glowing grip.
"Gotcha!" I yell, while you yank on my cap,
The fireflies dodge like they've all got a map.

Grass stains on knees and giggles abound,
As we dance round and round on the ground.
But don't step in poop — that's a minor detail,
We'll just laugh it off like a grand fairy tale.

Nestled in Nature's Embrace

A squirrel steals a sandwich right from my hands,
As birds join in on our picnic plans.
The ants march in like they own the place,
While we try to hide our food with grace.

A bug lands on my nose; now my face is a show,
You can't stop the giggles; oh look, there's a crow!
Under the trees, all we do is unwind,
Nature's got laughter and silliness entwined.

Between the Waves and the Whispering Trees

The ocean swells with a mighty roar,
While we lay back and settle for more.
A frisbee flies but gets caught in a breeze,
Plopping down hard between towering trees.

"Watch out!" someone shouts as we all take a dive,
We surface, laughing, feeling so alive.
The world's a playground, wild and absurd,
In this paradise, we're blissfully stirred.

Vistas of the Serene Coastline

Seagulls squawk, they take a dive,
Flip-flops dance, as we arrive.
Sunburned noses, oh what a sight,
Ice cream melting in the midday light.

Beach balls bounce, laughter rings,
A crab steals snacks, oh what a fling!
Sandy sandwiches, who needs a plate?
We'll just eat fast, before it's too late!

Cascade of Sapphire Dreams

Waves crash in with a playful splash,
Ronnie belly flops, what a big crash!
Surfers wobble on foam-topped waves,
While we search for our sunken graves.

Flip-flops flinging, the chase begins,
A piña colada spills on our chins.
Wigs fly off in the beachside breeze,
While sunbathers seek shade 'neath the trees.

Heartbeats on Ocean Breezes

Tiki torches light up the pathway,
Hula dancers twist in a quirky ballet.
Sand dollars hide while we search high and low,
Chasing after the tide like a goofy show.

Buckets and shovels forgotten, alas!
We find ourselves taking quite the class.
Learning the hula with two left feet,
Our instructor laughs as we skip and greet!

Lull of the Tropical Night

Stars glitter, like sprinkles on black,
Fireflies dance, they've got the knack.
Moonlight shines on a very loud frog,
Who's croaking out tunes from a soggy log.

Drinks in hand, we giggle and sway,
Laughter erupts, then fades away.
With every hiccup and cheerful cheer,
We toast to the nights we hold so dear!

Waves Crashing on Forgotten Paths

The waves are laughing, oh what fun,
   They tickle the toes of everyone.
  Forgotten paths of sand and sea,
    Lead to a world of silly glee.

  Seagulls gossip with the breeze,
  Swapping secrets with the trees.
A crab wearing shades strikes a pose,
 While a fish winks and off he goes.

Sandy snacks and coconut drinks,
   In this place, nobody stinks!
  A flip-flop thrown, a wild chase,
   Turns the shore into a race.

So let the waves erase your frown,
And follow the laughter all around.
With every splash, forget your strife,
  At this beach, you find new life.

Lost in the Lush Greenery

In thick green jungles, laughter reigns,
Where monkeys swing with funny brains.
Branches wave like they're in a dance,
While toucans yell, 'Give us a chance!'

A parrot squawks, claiming it's wise,
But trips on vines, what a surprise!
A sloth rolls by, moving so slow,
Too busy dreaming, don't you know?

With berries bouncing, colors bright,
Each step leads to pure delight.
A puddle splashes, friends do shout,
While a frog croaks, 'Let's dance about!'

Lost in lush greenery divine,
Each twist and turn worth your time.
Come join the fun, leave worries behind,
In this jungle, joy is easy to find.

The Dance of the Hibiscus

In the garden, blooms so gay,
Hibiscus sways, come join the play.
Petals twirl and shake in glee,
While bees buzz by, 'Just wait for me!'

A lizard grooves with flair so bold,
In shades of green and bits of gold.
The sun peeks in, a cheeky grin,
As flowers blush where they've been!

Dancing leaves in bright sunlight,
Waving at butterflies in flight.
A breeze kicks up, causing a thrill,
This party's fun, can't get your fill!

So come and join this dazzling dance,
The hibiscus will give you a chance.
With laughter and joy, understand,
In nature's embrace, you'll make a stand.

Mirage of the Moonlit Lagoon

At dusk, the lagoon wears a glow,
Reflections dance, putting on a show.
A frog winks under the silver beams,
While the fireflies weave light like dreams.

Water lilies float, dressed in grace,
Turns out, they've got quite the face!
'Hello there!' they cheer with delight,
'Join our party, it's outta sight!'

The moon's a jester, round and bright,
Making shadows that wiggle and bite.
A fish jumps high, a bouncy sprite,
Chasing its dreams in the moonlight.

So laugh and dance by the shimmering tide,
In this mirage, let joy be your guide.
When the sun returns, don't you fret,
The magic remains, you'll never forget.

Beneath the Coconut Canopy

In the shade where coconuts fall,
A monkey claims the beach ball.
With sunglasses on a funny face,
He's the king of this sandy place.

Palm fronds sway, a dancer's delight,
While sand crabs scuttle, quick in flight.
A towel battle begins to brew,
When seagulls swoop, just to steal a shoe.

Laughter echoes through the breeze,
From sunburnt tourists attempting to tease.
A pineapple hat sits askew,
As a dive into the sea turns into a brew.

So here we sip our coconut drinks,
And chuckle at life's silly kinks.
In the shade, our troubles cease,
Underneath nature's comedic lease.

Echoes of the Azure Sea

Waves that chuckle and play peek-a-boo,
Crashing softly, like a playful crew.
With beach balls flying all around,
And laughter symphonies profoundly sound.

A picnic blanket, a grand buffet,
Filled with snacks that seem to sway.
Seagulls eye the chips with glee,
Wings flapping in a comedic spree.

Footprints in the sand, a big parade,
As folks dance with an awkward charade.
A crab wearing shades moves with such flair,
While spectators cheer, without a care.

So take a dip or jump right in,
Let the water wash away your sin.
The sea knows jokes, oh can't you see?
In its azure embrace, we're wild and free.

Secrets of the Sunlit Cove

Hidden treasures in the cove,
Where flip-flops and funny hats rove.
A shy fish waves in its shy way,
While sunbathers melt in the midday.

Tiki torches dance with a flickering grin,
As someone attempts to belly flop in.
Splash! A wave crashes on a poor guy,
Drenched and droll, "I just want to dry!"

The sun casts shades of laughter bright,
While frisbees fly in a joyous flight.
Chasing shadows and running in glee,
A dog thinks the sea is its own spree.

Secrets of joy, in the waves that crash,
Silly moments caught in a flash.
For under the sun, we come alive,
Turning the mundane into a jive.

Journey to the Coral Oasis

Riding waves in a floaty boat,
With bamboo hats that surely gloat.
Fish in sunglasses glide on by,
While goofy dolphins leap and fly.

Maps with X's and silly lines,
Leading to treasure chests of limes.
We navigate with laughter bright,
Through ripples of fun, morning to night.

In this paradise, life's a jest,
Blending laughter with a beachy quest.
Lost flip-flops and a leaky cup,
We find our way just by looking up.

So grab a float and hold on tight,
To this journey filled with pure delight.
In coral hideaways where we all roam,
We'll laugh and play until it's home.

When the Horizon Calls Your Name

Paddle-boards race like ducks in a row,
While sunburnt tourists dance toe to toe.
Seagulls laugh at the snacks we forgot,
Chasing ice cream that melts on the spot.

Flip-flops fly in the sand, what a show,
As sunscreen battles the sun's fiery glow.
With a coconut drink, we're living the dream,
Except we still can't find the restroom, it seems.

In the Heart of the Green Maze

Lush leaves wave like they're saying hello,
We wander in circles—where did we go?
Machete in hand, we're jungle-bound fools,
Lost in a maze, but who needs those rules?

Monkeys throw coconuts; it's raining brown snacks,
As we trip over roots—hey, watch those attacks!
The guide said it's safe; we kinda believed,
But now all that's left is our sunburned reprieve.

Colorful Echoes of Island Life

Fish with neon stripes swim in a race,
While crabs in tuxedos try to keep pace.
The drinks are umbrella-ed, bright like a dream,
We cheers to the beach—a bubbly regime!

Flip-flop parades move down the hot shore,
As sandcastles crumble; oh, what a chore!
With shirts that say 'I need another piña,'
We giggle as waves crash with a loud 'see ya!'

Footsteps on Warm Sand

Wet feet leave trails in the golden expanse,
We dance with the waves in a heedless romance.
Towels like flags, we claim our small spot,
Except now the tide says we're all but forgot!

Sunscreen smudges make us look quite bizarre,
As we wave to a jellyfish drifting afar.
Oceanside picnics, culinary delight—
But ants RSVP'd; they put up a fight.

Enchantment of the Emerald Bay

There once was a crab in a hat,
Who danced with a fish on a mat.
They twirled in delight,
On a warm, starry night.

A seagull swooped down for a snack,
While a dolphin said, "Hey, watch your back!"
They laughed at the sun,
And all had their fun.

The turtles tried rollerblades too,
And the parrots sang tunes that they knew.
A party went wild,
Just like a child.

Then a beach ball flew through the air,
Landing right in a monkey's hair.
They chuckled and rolled,
In a day made of gold.

The Allure of Distant Shores

A hammock was set between two palms,
Where a sloth stretched out with his balms.
He sighed with a grin,
Sipping coconut gin.

A parrot squawked loudly, "Hey, friend!"
While a crab tried to sell him a blend.
"Smoothies! Fresh fare!"
The sloth just stood there.

A beach ball came bouncing along,
With a crab singing a silly song.
Together they played,
In this warm, sunny glade.

When the sun took a bow for the night,
The fireflies turned on their light.
They danced like a ball,
And had fun, one and all.

The Sun-Kissed Hideaway

In a treehouse so high, oh what a sight,
A monkey declared it the place of delight.
With snacks piled so high,
He said, "Just pass by!"

A lizard wore shades, looking cool,
While a bear in some water acted like a fool.
They splashed around,
And laughter unbound.

A tropical punch was served with flair,
As flamingos strutted without a care.
They danced in a row,
By a palm tree's glow.

The sun set like a big orange ball,
As crab friends decided to play catch ball.
They giggled and cheered,
With joy that they steered.

In Pursuit of Serene Skies

An octopus dreamed of a jetpack dream,
While a clam hoped to wake up supreme.
They plotted all night,
For a glorious flight.

A pineapple asked, "Can I join the crew?"
As a gull laughed and squawked, "I'll fly too!"
Together they soared,
While the beach mice roared.

A dolphin proposed a race to the sun,
With cheers from the crowd, 'This looks fun!'
They splashed in delight,
As they danced with the light.

When the stars came to twinkle above,
The friends gathered close and shared love.
With dreams made of cheer,
They laughed without fear.

Essence of the Mango Mirage

In a land where mangoes sway,
I once lost my hat to a fray.
The parrot laughed, took my drink,
And taught me to dance on the brink.

With each slice of fruit, I declare,
I might need a second chair.
My friends say I'm losing my touch,
But hey, those smoothies pack quite a punch!

The beach is a slippery surprise,
As I trip over sand, oh so wise.
The sun creeps low, what a sight,
I'll flip-flop dance into the night.

But amidst the chaos and cheer,
An iguana winks, drawing near.
Though life here seems quite absurd,
Laughing too hard, I lose my word.

Driftwood Dreams and Sunlit Shores

On driftwood I sit with my drink,
The ocean lets out a playful wink.
Seagulls compete for the best fry,
While I watch the clouds pass me by.

A crab joins in with a quick snap,
Making my snack turn into a trap.
I laugh as it strolls, so carefree,
This beach life seems perfect for me.

The sun wiggles and giggles around,
As I roll up my towel and roll down.
Sand in my toes, what a thrill,
Each wave seems to say, "Take your fill!"

But then comes a wave, bold and brash,
So I learn to swim, then I splash!
In this dream of driftwood galore,
I'll joyfully dive with laughter's roar.

Cascade of the Tropical Rainfall

A sprinkle of joy, then a pour,
Dancing in puddles is never a bore.
Umbrellas bloom like flowers in spring,
While I twirl, a mischievous fling.

Raindrops race down the palm tree leaves,
I chase after each one with ease.
They laugh as I slip on the floor,
A splash brings applause, oh what a chore!

With every drip, the laughter flows,
As I dodge puddles, strike a pose.
The sun peeks out, what a tease,
As I pirouette with wet, wild ease.

The stormy show came and went,
Yet in each drop, joy was lent.
With friends by my side, we all play,
Laughing at rain, what a silly day!

The Sun's Soft Melodies

The sun sings sweet tunes from on high,
While I snack on coconuts, oh my!
A crab tap dances to the beat,
And I join in on this sunny street.

With shades on tight, I sway to the sound,
Barefoot on sand, I glide around.
A random leap and a spin so fast,
I land in a pile of seaweed cast.

My friends point and giggle aloud,
As I dive straight into a crowd.
From warm laughs to splashes wide,
We're soaring through joy on this tide.

As music from shells softly plays,
I'm wrapped in a sunlit daze.
With melodies drifting, oh so free,
Life's a choral giggle by the sea!

The Scent of Fresh Rainfall

Puddles glisten like disco balls,
Kids in boots make joyful calls.
Umbrellas flipped, a comical sight,
Sliding in mud brings pure delight.

Raindrops tap on every roof,
Dancing ducks are most aloof.
Splashing here and giggling there,
Needless to say, clothes are wet wear!

Storm clouds gather, don't you fret,
Rainy days are the best, I bet.
We'll plot our next wild escapade,
As laughter pours, our worries fade.

When sun peeks out, we'll bask again,
Tell tales of mud and giggling rain.
Summer storms that bring us cheer,
In puddles, our happiness is near.

Where the Wildflowers Dance

Petals sway like dancers bright,
In fields of gold, what a sight!
Bees buzz by with silly grace,
Trying hard to keep their pace.

Sunshine kisses each flower's face,
While butterflies flit in a race.
Tall grass bows as the wind whirls,
Nature's stage in swirls and twirls!

Ladybugs wear their polka dots,
Picnic blankets and laughter spots.
Frogs croak cues from their grandstands,
Hopping along to nature's bands.

When twilight falls, stars peek shy,
Glow worms join the dance, oh my!
In this garden of whimsy and chance,
Life's a riot where flowers dance.

Stories Woven in Coral Reefs

Fishy tales beneath the waves,
A school of smiles that always braves.
Clownfish giggle, doing tricks,
Their goofy moves, a comedy flick.

Sea turtles glide with gentle grace,
Drifting slowly, a curious race.
Octopuses plotting their next prank,
Ink clouds burst, a spontaneous tank!

Crabs click-clack in a ballet of fun,
Stealing shells, oh what a run!
Jellyfish sway like floating lights,
Chasing currents through sparkling nights.

Anemones wave their feathery arms,
Whispers shared beneath the charms.
In coral circles, laughter weaves,
Nature's tales that nobody leaves.

A Serenade Beneath the Palms

Underneath the wavy fronds,
Laughter echoes, life responds.
Coconuts drop with a thud,
Playful antics in the sun's flood.

Hammocks sway as folks nap and dream,
While squirrels raid for fruit supreme.
A parrot squawks a cheeky tune,
Join the fun, don't be a loon!

Drinks with umbrellas, a funny sight,
Cocktails swirling, a toast to light.
Dancing shadows on golden sand,
Every giggle is simply grand!

As night falls, the stars spring out,
Flickering lights, a playful route.
With all the joy from sun to moon,
Life beneath palms sings a tune.

Celestial Drift in Caribbean Nights

Under the stars, we sail away,
Waves tickling toes, come what may.
A parrot squawks, gives a laugh,
While we sip rum, our joy's the path.

Sunburned noses, quite the sight,
Dance like fish in a moonlit night.
Flip-flops thrown, we skip the line,
To join the beach party, feeling fine.

Coconuts drop with a thud,
And mermaids giggle, it's all quite good.
We chase the tide with all our might,
With every wave, life's sheer delight.

But then the crabs start a parade,
Marching by, their little charade.
We join in step, it's quite absurd,
In our own show, we're such a herd!

Shades of Serenity by the Shore

Plenty of sun, my hat's awry,
Every time I laugh, a seagull flies.
My drink's a mystery, pineapple twist,
But finding a straw? It's hard to resist!

Footprints in sand, leading nowhere,
Chasing crabs, unaware of my hair!
The palm trees sway, sing a soft tune,
While I dance silly, beneath the moon.

Beach volleyball? A rickety game,
Serving a ball, it's never the same.
I dive to score, but land on my face,
Laughter erupts, I'm winning this race!

As day turns to night, the fireflies glow,
Friends gather 'round, there's laughter in tow.
With sand between toes and hearts so bold,
This silly escape is worth more than gold.

Pathways to the Sun-Drenched Isles

On sandy paths, we trip and tumble,
With flip-flops on, our laughter's humble.
The seagulls squawk, they steal our fries,
We wave good-bye, yet they don't shy.

A parrot squawks a joke or two,
With feathers bright, he joins our crew.
We dance like crabs, all sideways glee,
In this sun-soaked land, we're wild and free.

The ice cream drips, we gasp in fright,
The flavors blend, a comical sight.
We chase the waves, they tease and run,
A splash of joy, under the sun.

The palm trees sway, their leaves go "whoosh,"
We skip and spin, feeling like woosh!
With every giggle, we lose our cares,
A silly dance in sun-kissed air.

Reflections in Tropical Waters

In waters clear, our faces splash,
We check our hair, but oh, what a crash!
A fish flops by, gives us a wink,
While we laugh hard, probably stink.

The sun glints bright, we squint and grin,
Who knew relaxation could feel like sin?
With a floating drink, we drift in dreams,
While dancing sunbeams burst at the seams.

A crab steals snacks while we're distracted,
And for some reason, we're all impacted.
We chase him down, a silly sight,
As our laughs echo through the bright daylight.

The water glitters, oh, what a tease,
With every splash, we're caught with ease.
In this wild game of hide and seek,
Our laughter booms, uplifting, unique.

The Rhythm of the Warm Breeze

The wind whispers secrets, oh, what fun,
It tickles our noses, it races, it runs.
We sway like palm trees, a wobbly dance,
In breezy rhythms, we take a chance.

A coconut falls, we dive for cover,
Turns out it's just a playful lover.
We laugh as we dodge, oh what a sight,
In the warm breeze, everything's light.

The sun sets low, kissing the sea,
With fruity drinks, we shout "Yippee!"
We twirl around, forgetting the day,
With swaying bodies that shout "Hooray!"

The night brings crickets, they sing their tune,
While we chase stars, beneath the moon.
As laughter flows and time slips free,
In this breezy world, we just want to be.

Journey Through Bougainvillea

Down twisted paths where flowers bloom,
We spin through colors, dispelling gloom.
With petals bright, we wave and shout,
Who knew a flower could dance about?

A butterfly flutters, it steals the show,
We chase it down, our hearts all aglow.
But it veers left, we stumble and jolt,
In this flower-filled world, we laugh and bolt.

The foliage whispers a cheeky tease,
We giggle and wiggle, feeling the breeze.
A friendly squirrel tosses then runs,
As we giggle, he plays just for fun.

Under blooms so bright, we sip sweet tea,
Guided by laughter, wild and free.
In nature's embrace, our joy ignites,
Through bougainvillea, our laughter delights.

Odyssey Through the Silk Breezes

In a land where coconuts fall,
And flip-flops always call,
I chased a crab, thought it was neat,
But it scuttled away on tiny feet.

The sun's a massive ball of cheese,
That melts my worries with the breeze,
I found a parrot, bold and spry,
It mocked my dance; I can't deny!

With drinks adorned in fruit's embrace,
We laughed at seagulls' wild chase,
The hammock swayed, I took my nap,
Woke up to find my snack a trap!

So here I am, in this great plight,
Sunburned and itching from the bite,
But giggles rule in this warm land,
In paradise, I'm never bland!

Lullaby of the Ocean's Embrace

An octopus just stole my shoe,
It's wearing it now, who knew?
With sandy toes and barrel rolls,
I swear the fish are gossiping trolls!

A crab sang blues, not quite in tune,
It danced 'neath the sway of the moon,
The waves joined in, a choral feat,
My flip-flop took the lead with beat!

The palm trees sway, a rhythm grand,
They mock my moves, try as I stand,
With coconuts clapping in delight,
I fell over; it was quite the sight!

So while I dream of warm sea splashes,
The jellyfish giggle, making crashes,
In this lullaby where laughter flows,
Every wave tells tales no one knows!

Swaying Shadows of Paradise

In this land of once-tanned wights,
I lost my drink on bicentennial nights,
With glowing fruits I thought I'd sip,
Until a monkey made off with my chip!

The shadows dance, a crazy show,
Making shapes that steal the glow,
A lizard laughed, I swear it spoke,
Did it just call me an old bloke?

With beach balls bouncing left and right,
I'm dodging seagulls in flight,
I chased a breeze but caught a bug,
It stuck to me and gave a shrug.

So here we laugh, beneath the sun,
Playing silly games, all in fun,
In shadows swaying, light and free,
This paradise is where I must be!

Lost in the Hibiscus Fields

In hibiscus blooms, I've lost my way,
With petals whispering, 'Come and play!',
A bee buzzed loud, trying to tease,
I offered it snacks; it took a freeze!

The flowers swayed, a colorful mess,
Their laughter brightened my dull stress,
Each twist and turn, I felt so bold,
Until I tripped; now I'm just cold!

With sunshine spilling, a golden sea,
I danced with a turtle; how could it be?
I lost my shoe among the greens,
What sort of madness fit for queens?

So here I roam, a wandering fool,
In fields where petals form a pool,
While laughter rings and fun is real,
I've truly lost it—what a steal!

Island Whispers

A parrot squawked, what a noise,
He stole my hat, oh what joys!
The beachball bounced right off my nose,
As I chased crabs in my new toes.

A coconut fell with a thud,
Right on my foot, what a dud!
I danced with waves, took a quick dip,
But forgot to hold on to my flip-flip.

The sun draped rays like a great blanket,
While my drink was a fruity, wet spanket.
I slipped on sand like a slapstick clown,
And laughed so hard, I nearly drowned.

With each rum punch, my cares did flee,
While fish and turtles laughed at me.
A hammock swung, my heart took flight,
In this paradise, life feels just right.

Sandy Shores and Distant Dreams

On the sandy shores, slick and bright,
I found a crumpled map one night.
It led to treasures of jellybeans,
So sweet, they burst at the seams!

I built a castle, grand and wide,
But the tide soon was my castle's stride.
In came a wave, my fortress gone,
Now it's just a spot for a yawn.

Seagulls cackled, mocking my plight,
I threw them chips — a daring fight!
They swooped and dived, oh what a scene,
Distant dreams of snacks where I can glean.

But laughter filled the salty air,
I danced with sand, without a care.
My sunburned nose proudly demonstrated,
How summer fun just never waited.

Palm Fronds and Ocean Breezes

Beneath the palms, a breeze blew hot,
I flew my kite, but it got caught!
In palm fronds high, it tangled tight,
And made a monkey laugh so bright.

With sunglasses on, I tried to look cool,
But tripped on a child's forgotten pool.
Splash! A wave of squeals erupt,
And I was left flailing, all abrupt.

The fruit stand's offer was hard to resist,
A smoothie that did a hula twist.
But one sip revealed a strange taste,
Did the blender run, or was I too haste?

Yet laughter laced the salty air,
With ocean breezes tousling my hair.
In this chaos, joy took its hold,
And funny stories began to unfold.

Escaping the Ordinary

In my flip-flops, I made a dash,
Past a beach where quite the crowd would clash.
I sought adventure, so wild and strange,
But found myself on a merry-go-exchange.

A sunburned tourist, bright as a flame,
Kept asking me to join in their game.
We tossed a frisbee, it spun 'round and 'round,
Only to crash on the ground, with no sound.

The ice cream truck came, what a delight,
Until it broke down, oh what a plight!
We sang a tune, his cones on the floor,
While a crab crept by, wanting more.

But through the laughter, the memories made,
Normalcy fled, none could invade.
The ordinary vanished, replaced by cheer,
As waves whispered secrets, we stripped off fear.

Colorful Journeys in Paradise

A parrot danced in a straw hat,
Sipping juice, how funny is that!
Palm trees swayed with grace and flair,
Beach balls bouncing, flying through air.

Lizards lounged, sunglasses on proud,
Counting tourists, laughing out loud.
Flip-flops squeaked a playful tune,
Under the warm and lazy moon.

Sunsets painted the sea with glee,
While crabs played tag, oh what a spree!
Cocktails spilled on sandy shores,
Funny quirks behind wild closed doors.

A hammock strung so high, oh dear!
Fell down with a resounding cheer.
Laughter echoed through the strands,
Colorful journeys with open hands.

Tides of the Emerald Lagoon

Waves rolled in on a rubber raft,
Bumping hearts with every craft.
Silly seagulls stole our chips,
We chased them down with clownish flips.

Mermaids giggled, tails so bright,
Poking fun, oh, what a sight!
While fish threw parties, bubbles flew,
Mermaid wishes, just ask the crew!

Ocean's laughter tickled our toes,
As funny hats danced with the flows.
Starfish sporting cozy hats,
Swam with dolphins, and how they sat!

But when the waves began to sway,
We joined the sea in our wild play.
Emerald tides in a whirlpool spun,
A lagoon full of giggles, oh, such fun!

Dawn's Kiss on the Sandy Expanse

Morning broke with a silly grin,
Sunshine started the day to begin.
Birds in chorus, their songs a tease,
As palms bowed down in the soft breeze.

With coffee cups afloat on the waves,
We surfed the sunrise, acting like knaves.
Flip-flops flying, a fashion parade,
As beach towels turned into escapades!

A crab host welcomed with a small dance,
While we joined in with a wobbly prance.
Sand castles crumbled, a royal mess,
But laughter bloomed under morning's dress.

Dawn's kiss painted everything bright,
In this silly land of pure delight.
Oh, what magic in each grain of sand,
Where humor leads us hand in hand.

Footprints in the Lavender Sand

Lavender beach was a sight bizarre,
Flip-flops flying, no need for a car!
Footprints giggled, dancing with flair,
As sunscreen spread with a silly air.

Sandy toes played peek-a-boo,
With waves that came just to say boo!
Kites above looked like jelly beans,
Painting the sky with colorful scenes.

A picnic spread with mismatched plates,
Where baked beans decided our fates.
Seagulls swooped for an overdue snack,
Then peered at us with a comic knack.

With hearts so light, we chased the sun,
Our footprints faded, but oh, what fun!
In lavender dreams, our laughter would land,
Found joy in traces of footprints in sand.

Serenity Beneath the Sunset Palms

Beneath the palms, the laughter flows,
Where sandy shores hide all our woes.
With ice-cold drinks in hand we bide,
While seagulls squawk and shrimpsters glide.

The sun dips low, the sky ablaze,
We dance like waves in goofy ways.
Flip-flops flying, hats askew,
Who knew sunburn might bring such goo?

A crab with style struts with pride,
While jellyfish take the fast slide.
We giggle as they float on by,
"Who's next for joy?" we squeal and cry.

In this paradise where troubles cease,
With rubber ducks, we find our peace.
Under the stars, so bright, so grand,
We share our dreams upon the sand.

Floating on a Sea of Tranquility

In a pool of dreams, we find delight,
With flamingo floats, we take flight.
The sun a spotlight on our show,
As we somersault and waddle slow.

Splashing around with wayward grace,
The ducks join in, a silly race.
The water's warm, the laughs are loud,
As we make fun of the cloud crowd.

A beach ball bounces, heads all sway,
"Catch it now!" we shout and play.
Laughter echoes, a bubbly cheer,
As all our cares just disappear.

With snacks galore and sun-kissed skin,
We lounge like lobsters, bright and thin.
The floaties cheer, the sun agrees,
Life's best joys are found with ease.

Whispers of the Emerald Isles

On emerald shores where breezes tease,
We sip our drinks with mighty ease.
The parrots squawk in color bright,
While we discuss what's wrong or right.

A crab negotiation on the sand,
"Three fries for peace!" it makes a stand.
We chuckle hard, it's quite the sight,
As shells rattle in the moonlit night.

With coconut hats and tiki garb,
We strike a pose, then take a barb.
"Look at me!" we laugh and prance,
A limbo fight becomes our dance.

But soon the tides will pull us back,
Our giggles swept along the track.
Yet echoes of our joyful spree,
Will linger on, sweet memory.

Solstice in the Coconut Grove

In groves of coconuts, wild and free,
We find the quirkiest jubilee.
A limbo stick, a dance so grand,
While fruity drinks are close at hand.

The monkeys swing while we attempt,
To understand this silly event.
Straws in our drinks like funky hats,
We giggle at the dance of bats.

The sun glows bright, the palm trees sway,
As we declare it "Silly Day!"
With ukuleles strumming tunes,
Under the light of glowing moons.

Though time may fly, we won't forget,
The laughter had, no cause for regret.
In this paradise of joy and cheer,
We'll always find a path back here.

Reflections of the Vast Horizon

A beach ball bounces by so fast,
With sunburned folks, they laugh and gasp.
Flip-flops fly like birds in flight,
Chasing waves with all their might.

Pineapple drinks with tiny straws,
Remind us that we're here because!
The sand between our toes feels grand,
But now it's stuck, oh what a plan!

Sunscreen battles leaves us pale,
While seagulls steal our lunch with zeal.
Under umbrellas, we plot and scheme,
To catch the sun, or so it seems!

As all is said and all is done,
Its pure, comedic, endless fun.
With laughter echoing on the shore,
We'll keep on playing forevermore!

Rose-Colored Skies at Dusk

The sunset paints the sky in hues,
As flip-flops clash with every cruise.
A crab with flair, he struts around,
Claiming ownership of the ground.

Laughter spills like water's edge,
While ice cream melts from every ledge.
A dance-off breaks, the crowd draws near,
Two left feet and lots of cheer!

The palm trees sway like funky dancers,
We lose our hats, and take our chances.
While jellyfish play hide and seek,
"Watch the waves!" we cry, "Don't peek!"

As night descends, we roast marshmallows,
With cheeky jokes and silly fellows.
In rose-colored dreams, we twirl and glide,
Creating memories that cannot hide!

Echoes from the Island Heart

A parrot squawks a joke or two,
While fellow tourists yell, "Yoo-hoo!"
Bamboo huts and cheer all round,
With dancing feet that won't calm down.

Flip-flop races on burning sand,
The finish line? No one had planned!
Grinning wide, we all collide,
In fits of giggles, we can't abide.

The locals smile and roll their eyes,
At our oceanic, silly tries.
Mango tarts set hearts ablaze,
A fruit parade that always stays.

As the drums begin to play tonight,
We shake it off and feel just right.
With echoes ringing in the air,
This joyous moment, beyond compare!

Mysteries of the Calm Waters

The ocean gleams like crystal ball,
But watch your step, or you might fall!
A family of fish gives us a grin,
As snorkelers gasp, and then dive in.

Bubbles rise with every laugh,
While beach umbrellas wobbly craft.
A friendly dolphin waves hello,
As beachgoers prepare to show!

Sandcastles rise with buckets loud,
Only to be flattened by a crowd.
Waterslides become a race,
With seagulls rooting for our pace.

As evening falls and stars appear,
We choose our favorite souvenir.
With laughter echoes on the shore,
The mysteries linger, forevermore!

Canvas of the Dusk's Embrace

A coconut fell right on my head,
I laughed so hard, almost wedged.
Waves crashed in, like uninvited guests,
While seagulls stole my lunch, no rest.

Flip-flops squeaked on the sandy beach,
Dancing crabs had a new friend to teach.
With each sip of my fruity drink,
I spilled it all, and couldn't think.

Sunset painted skies, what a sight,
No filter needed, pure delight.
A parrot squawked in a bright parade,
While I attempted to catch a shade.

Laughter echoed, the stars appeared,
A beach blanket, still unsteered.
With every flop and laugh I made,
This salty life, I gladly paid.

Vibrant Hues of Island Retreats

Pink flamingos, strutting tall,
In my flip-flops, I risked a fall.
Every color burst in my drink,
As I sat down, began to sink.

Palm trees swayed, bending low,
While I danced like no one would know.
A parrot mimicked my silly song,
Made me wonder where I went wrong.

Surfboards lined like a gang of pals,
While I slipped and fell, oh—the howls!
Wave after wave, I tried to stand,
Might as well make things a bit planned.

A sunburned nose and a goofy grin,
Chasing seagulls, I could win.
In this paradise, I found my groove,
With laughter shared, I started to move.

Echoes of the Seabreeze

Whispers of the sea, they call my name,
Though I swear, it's just a beach game.
Sandy toes and a messy bun,
Who knew all day could be such fun?

The tide rolled in, with a cheeky wink,
A wave knocked me down, oh how I think!
Shells like treasures, I gathered fast,
But tripped on a fish, oh what a blast!

Sipping piña coladas with wild flair,
A crab just pinched my sandy hair.
Shell collecting turned into a sport,
With my new friends, I'll never be caught.

Evenings lit by stringed beach lights,
As we danced away, oh what delights!
Who knew fun could be this cheap,
With laughter spilled, I lost all sleep.

Chasing Rainbows in the Heat

A rainbow drink, so bright and bold,
But spilled it all, oh, what a hold!
Curly straws waved like a parade,
And all my worries began to fade.

Heat hugs tight, but I don't mind,
With goofy games, new joys I find.
Chasing through colors of ice cream treats,
While dodging the ants on quick little feet.

A hula hoop dared me to play,
But it rolled away—oh, what a day!
I chased it down, caught a sunbeam,
An island life, it can't be a dream.

Under stars, we shared our tales,
Of quirky wishes and laughing fails.
In every sip and sunny glee,
I found a place I long to be.

Lullabies in the Coconut Canopy

Swinging high in leafy beds,
A squirrel sings with nutty threads.
Palm fronds sway like dancers bold,
While dreams of fruit in slumber rolled.

Kookaburra's laugh rings clear,
While sleepy ants are drawing near.
Coconuts fall with a thud and crack,
The night brings snacks, but none come back!

Lizards play, they strut their stuff,
In this world, it's never tough.
Under stars, we share a jest,
As dreams come true, we take our rest.

With coconuts as pillows found,
We snooze away with joyous sound.
In this lush, vibrant leafy space,
Lullabies bring a smile to the place.

Murmurs of the Ocean's Whisper

Waves roll in with a cheeky grin,
Jellyfish waltzing, let's begin.
Seagulls squawk, a salty feat,
Chasing crabs on scampering feet.

Shells whisper secrets to the sand,
While flip-flops play on seaweed strands.
A dolphin winks, it knows the joke,
As sandcastles bend and almost choke.

Like a clam with pearls, so tight,
Hiding treasures out of sight.
The ocean sings a silly song,
Where everyone belongs, along.

In fleeting tides, our laughter sways,
With every splash, we count the days.
The shoreline's call, a breeze to share,
In the ocean's laugh, we find our care.

Captured in a Tropical Sunset

The sun dons shades of orange and pink,
While flamingos strut and flirt and wink.
A parrot squawks a slangy phrase,
As we marvel at the sky's warm blaze.

With piña coladas in coconut cups,
We cheer the dusk while the laughter erupts.
As the goats on the hillside take their stroll,
A sunset paints the world, a dazzling bowl.

Swaying to rhythms of calypso tunes,
Beneath the light of shining moons.
Friends here gather, what a funny lot,
With jokes that bubble and never rot.

Cheers to moments that make us grin,
As twilight dances, it's time to begin.
With colors that blend, shadows take flight,
We capture the laughter, igniting the night.

À La Mer: Voyage of the Heart

A boat sails off with a giddy cheer,
With snacks and jokes for all to hear.
The captain spills soup; it's over the side,
As fish come up thinking we've lied.

We swap our hats to catch a breeze,
While sunburn laughter is sure to please.
The ocean's tales are full of snacks,
With mermaids giggling at our hijacks.

Flotsam dreams and jetty wishes,
Under the sun, we feast on swishes.
Each wave is a step of joyous art,
In every splash, we mend the heart.

So raise a glass to salty glee,
We hoot and holler, just you and me.
This journey's wild, the wind in our hair,
A heart-light voyage, beyond compare.

Dance of the Ginger Blossom

In a hut where coconuts sway,
Ginger blooms laugh, come out to play.
They twirl and spin under sun's bright gleam,
Bumbling bees join the sweet daydream.

The parrot tries to steal the show,
With disco moves, he puts on quite a glow.
While the iguana, cool in shades,
Takes selfies, as the party cascades.

A monkey swings from vine to vine,
Flipping snacks, he's feeling fine.
Laughter erupts, joins the breeze,
As they dance beneath the swaying trees.

The night falls soft, the stars ignite,
Dancing ginger won't stop tonight.
With a wink, the moon joins too,
In this tropical fiesta, for me and you.

Reflections in the Aqua Abyss

Dipping toes in bluest waves,
Laughing fish with tiny knaves.
They splash and play, all quite absurd,
A dolphin sings, or so I've heard.

Crabs in shorts strut down the beach,
Pretending they're the latest speech.
While seagulls caw, like a whole crew,
Stealing fries; oh what can you do?

A sunburned tourist with a grin,
Forgets the sunscreen, now is a sin.
As a wave rolls in, all fun and glee,
His beach ball flies, setting them free.

The sunset dances, colors explode,
In giggly waves, they hit the road.
In the depths of the aqua's fun mine,
We find smiles where the sea meets wine.

Pathways Through the Coral Wilds

Waves crash down, a salty twist,
In coral kingdoms, we can't resist.
Clownfish giggle at silly sights,
We join in too, what a delight!

Seahorses parade, dressed up so fine,
With tiny tuxedos, they shine divine.
Eels pull pranks, a slippery crew,
While starfish laugh at their own view.

Lobsters bake in the ocean heat,
Dance to rhythms, tapping their feet.
As the turtles spin, doing a glide,
In underwater parties, they take pride.

The reef's a stage, each fin a flair,
In the wilds of color, nothing's rare.
So join the wave, it's time for fun,
In pathways through oceans, we've all just begun!

Mosaic of Mango Dreams

Under palm trees, mangoes drop,
Juicy dancers, they never stop.
They tango on the kitchen floors,
While laughter spills from open doors.

Tropical smoothies blend like charm,
Bringing sweetness, no need for harm.
With a splash of rum and twinkling eyes,
We craft concoctions, oh what a prize!

Lemons compete with mangoes' grace,
Trying hard to take their place.
But those juicy gems just laugh and sway,
Winning hearts at the fruit buffet.

At night, we toast to the golden hue,
Mangoes rule, and they can woo.
In this mosaic of flavor and cheer,
Life's a party when mangoes are near!

A Sojourn of Colorful Horizons

In hammock dreams, I gently sway,
With a coconut smile, keeping woes at bay.
Palm trees dance in a comedic show,
While seagulls squawk their wobbly flow.

Sandy toes and sunburnt cheeks,
Chasing crabs as my laughter peaks.
I slip and trip on a limbo stick,
And tumble down in a silly flick.

Beneath a sky of cotton candy blue,
I lose my drink, what a sticky brew!
A parrot jokes, 'You're dancing wrong,'
But who cares? I'm humming a happy song.

With every splash, the ocean teases,
Fish join in, dancing in breezy eases.
With bright horizons, I'll never rest,
Just soaking in life's goofy fest.

Swaying to the Island Rhythm

On a boat made of banana leaves,
I set sail with laughter, and no one grieves.
The captain's a monkey, swinging with flair,
While I chuckle at the ocean's wild stare.

Crab races happen when the sun's too bright,
Each crustacean chases with all of their might.
But I trip on sand, and oh, what a sight!
The beach cheers me on, it's sheer delight.

In a tight sarong, I twist and I twirl,
With a hula hoop made of bright sea pearl.
My inner rhythm is so out of tune,
But the fish all clap, it's a party too soon!

Amidst coconut trees, my worries blend,
I dance with the tide, no need to pretend.
With the sun going down, I laugh with desire,
For this wacky life is a never-ending choir.

Uncharted Waters of the Heart

In the splash of the surf, my heart does flutter,
Searching for treasure, I find only butter.
A whale grins wide, offers me a hand,
"We like it quirky, join our band!"

Love is a fish that slips through my grasp,
Like jellyfish hugs that make me gasp.
I throw out my net; it's all in vain,
But laughing with dolphins eases my pain.

Under the moon's glow, we dance on the tide,
With seaweed garlands, we let love slide.
The stars above wink as we mr. sea-star,
And the jelly-like jellyfish cheer from afar.

In the game of love, I make silly moves,
With flippers on feet, nobody approves!
Yet in this ocean of laughter and cheer,
I find my heart's song, perfectly clear.

Glistening Sand and Hidden Trails

On paths of gold, I stumble and fall,
Covered in sunscreen, my laughter's a call.
I chase after shells, like a spy on a quest,
Only to find out they're all just a jest.

A crab gives chase, "Hey, don't you dare!"
It sets my heart racing in the warm air.
With flip-flops flapping, I run in a swirl,
As sea breezes giggle, my hair starts to curl.

I stop to sip a mocktail of glee,
The umbrella's crooked, it's hard to see.
Seagulls swoop down and swipe at my drink,
And I laugh as I start to splash and blink.

With paths uncharted and laughter as my guide,
I find my way with a joyful stride.
For each grain of sand brings an echo of cheer,
In this crazy journey, nothing to fear!

Secrets of the Sunlit Shore

On sandy plots where seagulls dance,
I tripped and fell, what an old romance!
My flip-flops flew into the breeze,
As laughter echoed through the trees.

The sun's a friend that's always bright,
But it gives my nose a funny fright!
I wore a hat that looked quite grand,
But it flew away across the sand.

We built a castle, tall and proud,
Till waves snuck in, oh that was loud!
The crab brigade came out to play,
Deciding a snack was the best way.

Bikini top that barely clung,
Left my dear friend feeling young!
With laughter, joy, and sun so bold,
The stories of our trip unfold.

Journey to the Palm Haven

Beneath the palms, we sought some shade,
But found a spot quite poorly laid!
A picnic feast, oh what delight,
Till ants arrived, oh what a sight!

A coconut fell, took aim at Dave,
He ducked and rolled, oh how we gave!
The juice erupted, a splashy hit,
We laughed so hard, we almost split.

And then came llamas, quite bizarre,
Wearing sunglasses, like they're stars!
They posed for photos, such a scene,
I think I'll call them Llama Jean!

With friends like these, we can't go wrong,
Our escapade was pure and strong.
Palm haven dreams with giggles stored,
Adventure here we can't afford!

Serenade of the Sapphire Sea

The ocean sings a merry tune,
While fish dance near the silver moon.
A jellyfish gave me quite a scare,
But really, it just wanted to share!

We spotted a dolphin with flair and tricks,
But all it did was show us its six!
Flipping and flopping with all its might,
It giggled at us, a funny sight!

With sunburned noses and sand-filled shoes,
We made the best of our funny blues.
Oh, how the waves pulled at our feet,
With each splash, life's rhythm felt sweet!

The sapphire sea, a jester's stage,
With fish as actors, the world's a page.
And as we laughed 'neath the sun's embrace,
We found our hearts in this silly place.

Lush Horizons and Golden Skies

In a land of lush and golden hue,
I wore a shirt with a wild view.
The parrots squawked, as if to tease,
While I danced badly to a gentle breeze.

Horizon wide, my eyes went wide,
For I had just lost my favorite ride!
An inflatable llama, bright and pink,
Drifting away, I was on the brink!

Chasing it down, I slipped and fell,
In mud and laughter, oh what a smell!
We caught the llama, soaked and free,
It giggled at me, oh silly spree!

With sunsets painted all in fun,
Our laughter echoed, every pun.
In a paradise where joy won't die,
We lived our dreams beneath the sky.

The Enchanted Palm Path

Beneath the swaying palms they sway,
I step on sand in a silly way.
Coconuts tumble, birds take flight,
My hat flies off, oh what a sight!

The monkeys laugh with their cheeky grins,
As I trip over my flip-flop sins.
A crab gives chase, it's quite the race,
I laugh and wave in my clumsy space.

The sun above is a playful tease,
It warms my back, it feels like cheese.
I dance with waves, clumsy and free,
In this paradise, just let it be!

With a wink, the palm trees sway,
Inviting all to join in play.
So grab your fun, come out and cheer,
Life's a beach, let's all shift gear!

Secrets of Sunset's Palette

Crayons in the sky, colors collide,
Paintbrush strokes where the sun likes to hide.
I sip my drink, with a slice of lime,
A parrot squawks, amplifying chime.

Swipe my hand in hues of bright orange,
As that cheeky monkey starts to forage.
Pink clouds giggle, teasing the day,
While surfboards race, imagination at play.

The horizon grins, it's a cheeky prank,
Like a piñata bursting with shades of dank.
A laugh escapes, amidst soft waves,
This sunset party, how it behaves!

Even the stars join in the fun,
Winking down, "Can we be one?"
With splashes of laughter, under moon's guile,
In this sunset palette, we'll stay for a while!

Paradise Found Through the Canopy

Up in the trees, the squirrels chatter,
I swing from vines, just like a spatter.
The leaves tickle me, a giggly treat,
As I plummet down with flailing feet.

My guide—a toucan, bright and bold,
Says, "Follow me, it's a story to be told!"
I trip on roots, but what a thrill,
In this jungle maze, my heart won't chill.

Laughter echoes as I dodge a snake,
Is that a vine or a playful mistake?
The monkeys cheer; they throw banana peels,
As I skoot on by, they're spinning my wheels.

Branches sway, the sun plays peek-a-boo,
"Join our dance!" calls the frog in the blue.
So through the canopy, we'll laugh and twirl,
In this paradise, life's a wild whirl!

Embrace of Warm Winds

The breeze tickles my nose, oh what a tease,
While I try to balance on the swaying knees.
A kite takes off, and I try my best,
But I end up tangled, a quirky mess.

The gulls flock by, with raucous squawks,
As sunscreen drips while I take a walk.
A beach ball rolls, ready for a dance,
I chase it down, not quite by chance.

Warm winds whisper, carrying giggles,
As I juggle shells, making silly wiggles.
A sunburn laugh across my bright face,
In this warm embrace, I find my place.

Lemonade spills while I twist and spin,
My friends all join — the chorus begins.
So in these winds, let's frolic and sway,
Embracing the fun, come out and play!

Journey through Nature's Palette

In a field so bright, a cow did wear,
A rainbow hat that made folks stare.
He danced and pranced, oh what a sight,
Chasing butterflies that took to flight.

A parrot squawked, with colors bold,
Claimed he was a treasure, worth more than gold.
He tried to sell seashells, just for a laugh,
But folks just chuckled and took a photograph.

The river giggled, with frogs that played,
Competitions to leap, where dreams were laid.
A turtle complained, he was always late,
His shell wasn't a car; oh, isn't fate great?

Beneath the trees, a picnic spread wide,
With ants in tuxedos, they danced side by side.
They served up fruit, made hats from leaves,
And when they were full, they rolled up their sleeves.

Glimmers of the Sea at Twilight

Upon the shore, the fish had a chat,
Pondering why humans wear a hat.
They'd try it too, but it fell with a plop,
And then they chuckled as they swam non-stop.

A crab claimed he'd found a gold ring,
Turns out it was just a soda can's bling.
It sparkled and shined; he strutted with pride,
Until it rolled away, 'Oh, ocean, be my guide!'

The breeze carried whispers from far-off lands,
Where sunbathers fanned themselves with bright hands.
A seagull swooped down, for a snack on the sand,
But snatched a hot dog, oh isn't life grand?

As twilight invited the stars to twinkle,
A clam laughed aloud; it took quite a crinkle.
The ocean giggled and danced in its wave,
For every night is a sea critter's rave.

Whispers of the Ocean's Heart

The starfish held court with tales quite absurd,
About a fish who claimed he could fly like a bird.
The other sea critters rolled 'round with glee,
For even the jellyfish knew it was a spree.

A dolphin flipped tales of great underwater games,
Synchronized swimming and outrageous names.
He made them laugh 'til they rolled in the foam,
Then raced with a shrimp, who just stayed at home.

At sunset, the octopus donned a top hat,
Declaring himself as the ocean's diplomat.
He waved at the boats that wobbled and shook,
"Will you join my party?" oh, how that fishhook!

And so they all danced in the ocean so blue,
Where laughter flowed freely, and troubles were few.
The whispers of joy echoed far and wide,
In this sea of delight, where all friends abide.

Bliss in the Tropical Breeze

In a hammock strung tight between two palm trees,
Lies a man with a drink; oh, how he does squeeze.
He tries for a nap, but bugs buzz around,
With antics so funny, they just won't back down.

The monkeys above play a grand little jest,
Flinging coconuts at the man's eager chest.
He dodges and weaves like a dance on the ground,
While laughing out loud at the fun that he's found.

The waves of the beach brought sandcastles tall,
Built by little feet, they soon had a fall.
With every new wave, more giggles would rise,
As they splashed around, it was all a surprise.

The sun gradually sets, a burst of warm rays,
And laughter still echoes as they end the day.
For bliss in the breeze brings a smile so true,
In this whimsical land, where friends are the crew.

www.ingramcontent.com/pod-product-compliance
Lightning Source LLC
Chambersburg PA
CBHW072128070526
44585CB00016B/1572